HEINEMANN GUIDED

BEGINNER LE

JANE AUSTEN

Northanger Abbey

Retold by Florence Bell

HEINEMANN

BEGINNER LEVEL

Series Editor: John Milne

The Heinemann Guided Readers provide a choice of enjoyable reading material for learners of English. The series is published at five levels – Starter, Beginner, Elementary, Intermediate and Upper. At **Beginner Level**, the control of content and language has the following main features:

Information Control

The stories are written in a fluent and pleasing style with straightforward plots and a restricted number of main characters. The cultural background is made explicit through both words and illustrations. Information which is vital to the story is clearly presented and repeated where necessary.

Structure Control

Special care is taken with sentence length. Most sentences contain only one clause, though compound sentences are used occasionally with the clauses joined by the conjunctions 'and', 'but', and 'or'. The use of these compound sentences gives the text balance and rhythm. The use of Past Simple and Past Continuous Tenses is permitted since these are the basic tenses used in narration and students must become familiar with these as they continue to extend and develop their reading ability.

Vocabulary Control

At **Beginner Level** there is a controlled vocabulary of approximately 600 basic words, so that students with a basic knowledge of English will be able to read with understanding and enjoyment. Help is also given in the form of vivid illustrations which are closely related to the text.

For further information on the full selection of Readers at all five levels in the series, please refer to the Heinemann Readers catalogue.

Contents

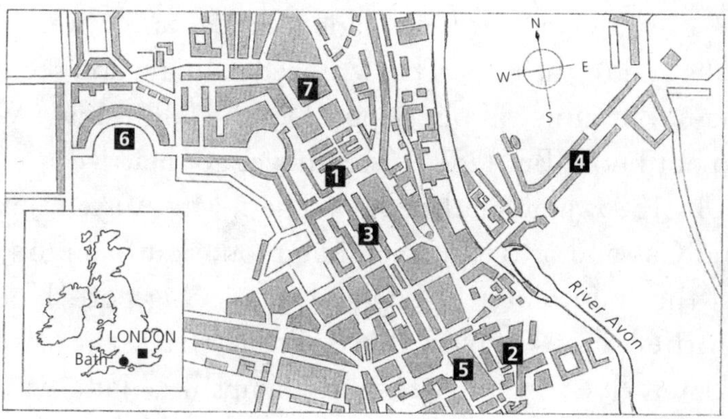

Bath: **1** Edgar's Buildings **2** Lower Rooms **3** Milsom Street **4** Pulteney Street **5** Pump Room **6** The Crescent **7** Upper Rooms (Assembly Rooms)

A Note About the Author

Jane Austen was born on 16th December 1775. She lived in the village of Steventon, in Hampshire, in the south of England. Her father was the clergyman of the church in Steventon. Jane had six brothers and one sister – Cassandra.

From 1782 to 1784 Jane and Cassandra lived at a school. From 1785, Jane's father taught the girls at home. Jane learnt English literature, English language, French, Italian and music. She read poetry and novels.

Jane's brother, Edward, lived with Thomas and Catherine Knight. Mr and Mrs Knight had a large house – Godmersham Park – in Kent. Jane and her sister often visited Edward at Godmersham Park.

From 1801, the Austens lived in Bath, in the south-west of England. In Bath, Jane and Cassandra went to balls and to theatres. They enjoyed dancing and seeing plays. But Jane was not happy. Did she fall in love? We do not know. But Jane Austen never got married.

In 1805, Jane's father died. Then, Mrs Austen, Jane and Cassandra lived in Southampton. Southampton is on the south coast of England. It is a big port. Jane's brother, Frank, lived there. From 1810, the three women lived in Chawton, in Hampshire. Jane wrote letters and books. Cassandra took care of the house. They visited their brothers and their families. Jane Austen was a kind, intelligent and amusing woman. She often laughed.

In 1816, Jane Austen became ill. Cassandra took care of her. Jane died on 18th July 1817. She was 41 years old.

Jane Austen did not write many books. But she is one of the most famous British writers. Her novels are: *Sense and Sensibility* (1811), *Pride and Prejudice* (1813), *Mansfield Park* (1814) and *Emma* (1816). *Northanger Abbey* and *Persuasion* (1818) were published after Jane Austen had died. Millions of people have read her books. Many films have been made of her stories.

A Note About This Story

Time: 1802. **Place**: Bath, in the south-west of England.

Jane Austen wrote about people in English Society. These people had money, houses and land. They did not work. They visited each others' houses. They played cards and they read books. They went to balls and to theatres in the towns. They rode horses in the country. Or they drove in their carriages. The carriages were pulled by fine horses.

In the eighteenth century, books of horror-stories were popular. These horror-stories were about old, dark houses. The houses had frightening ghosts or spirits in them! And there were old, dark trees in the gardens! Young women often read these frightening stories.

The city of Bath was very popular in the seventeenth and eighteenth centuries. Springs of hot water came up from the ground. People came to Bath. They drank this special water and they washed themselves in it. The water was a medicine. In the winter, thousands of people left London and other big cities. They stayed in Bath for a few months. They wore beautiful clothes and jewels. And they went to grand balls and to the theatres. All the young women wanted to meet rich and handsome young men.

People drank the spring water in the Pump Room. They met their friends and they talked. There were balls in the Assembly Rooms. These were two buildings with large rooms, or salons, where people met. One building was in the north of the city – the Upper Rooms. The Lower Rooms were in the south of the city. People danced. They ate good food and they played cards for money. The Royal Crescent was a popular place too. People walked along this beautiful street in Bath. They looked at the fine buildings.

At this time, people spoke very politely. They often used the names Mr, Miss or Mrs. Young women did not go out alone. It was not correct. Young women were introduced to young men. After that, they could talk to them.

The People in This Story

Mr Allen
ˈmɪstə(r) ˈælən

Mrs Allen
ˈmɪsɪz ˈælən

Catherine Morland
ˈkæθrɪn ˈmɔːlənd

James Morland
dʒeɪmz ˈmɔːlənd

Mrs Thorpe
ˈmɪsɪz θɔːp

Isabella Thorpe
ˈɪzəbelə θɔːp

Maria and Anne Thorpe
məˈrɪə(r) ənd æn θɔːp

John Thorpe
dʒɒn θɔːp

Henry Tilney
ˈhenrɪ ˈtilniː

Eleanor Tilney
ˈelenə ˈtilniː

General Tilney
ˈdʒenrəl ˈtilniː

Captain Frederick Tilney
ˈkæptɪn ˈfredrɪk ˈtilniː

Mr and Mrs Morland
ˈmɪstə(r) ənd ˈmɪsɪz ˈmɔːlənd

1

Catherine Goes to Bath

It was January 1802. Miss Catherine Morland was very excited. She was going to stay in the city of Bath for six weeks. She was going to stay with her friends, Mr and Mrs Allen.

'Bath is a beautiful city,' Mrs Allen said. 'We will enjoy ourselves in Bath, Catherine. The best people in Society will be there. We will dance at balls and we will go to plays.'

'Will I meet a handsome young man?' Catherine asked herself.

Catherine Morland was seventeen years old. She was a pretty, happy girl. She was slim and she had dark curly hair.

Catherine lived with her family in the village of Fullerton. Her father was the clergyman of the church.

It was the day of the journey. Catherine put her clothes in leather cases. Her mother helped her.

'Take some warm clothes,' Mrs Morland said. 'The nights will be cold!'

Soon, everything was ready. Mr Morland gave his daughter some money. Catherine got into the Allens' carriage. She said goodbye to her family. And Catherine Morland started on her journey to Bath!

2

Catherine's New Friends

The Allens had an apartment in Pulteney Street, near the centre of Bath. Catherine loved the city. She loved the wide streets, the big houses and the shops. The streets of Bath were crowded with people. And the shops were full of beautiful things.

In the evenings, people went to balls. There were balls in the large buildings called the Upper Rooms and the Lower Rooms. In the mornings, many people went to the Pump Room. They drank the water. And they met their friends.

There were many things to do in Bath. Catherine was very happy.

It was Friday evening. The Allens took Catherine to the Lower Rooms. The Rooms were crowded. People were eating, talking and dancing in the salons.

Mrs Allen and Catherine sat down together in a large salon. Mr Allen walked through the crowded room. Catherine wanted to dance. But she did not have a dancing-partner. Soon, Mr Allen returned, and there was a tall young man with him. He introduced the young man to Catherine.

'This is Mr Henry Tilney,' Mr Allen said. 'I know his father. But I have not seen him for a long time. The Tilneys live at Northanger Abbey.'

Henry Tilney bowed to Catherine. He was a very handsome man. He was about twenty-five years old.

'Will you be my partner for the next dance, Miss Morland?' he asked.

Catherine bowed. Mr Tilney held her hand and they started to dance. Catherine was very happy. She was dancing with a handsome young man! At the end of the dance, the young people sat down together.

'Do you know Bath well, Mr Tilney?' Catherine asked.

'I have visited Bath many times,' Mr Tilney replied. 'But I am the clergyman of a church many miles away.'

Mr Tilney smiled at Catherine. 'Now I must ask you some questions,' he said.

Catherine laughed. 'What questions?' she asked.

Mr Tilney smiled again and he spoke quickly.

'Have you been in Bath long? Have you been to the Upper Rooms? Have you been to the theatre? Do you like Bath? These are my questions,' Mr Tilney said.

'I have been in Bath for a week,' said Catherine. 'My answer to the other questions is, yes!' And she laughed again.

'You are laughing at me!' said Mr Tilney. 'Will you write about me in your diary tonight?'

'I don't write in a diary,' Catherine said.

'I do not believe that. Every young girl writes in a diary,' Mr Tilney said. 'Many things will happen to you in Bath. You must remember all of them!'

The next morning, Catherine and Mrs Allen went to the Pump Room. Mr Tilney was not at the Pump Room. But Mrs Allen saw a friend. She had not met her friend, Mrs Thorpe, for many years.

'Mrs Thorpe!' said Mrs Allen. 'I haven't seen you for fifteen years!'

'My dear Mrs Allen,' Mrs Thorpe replied. 'I am very happy to see you! Here are my three daughters. This is Isabella. She is the eldest. Isn't she beautiful? And here are Maria and Anne.'

'And this is Miss Catherine Morland,' said Mrs Allen.

'Miss Morland?' Isabella asked. She looked at Catherine. 'Are you the sister of Mr James Morland? Mr Morland is the friend of my brother, John. They are both students at Oxford University. James stayed with us at Christmas.'

Soon, Catherine and Isabella were talking happily. Isabella was four years older than Catherine and she was very beautiful. She was wearing fine, fashionable clothes.

Isabella knew Bath well. She talked to Catherine about the balls. And she told her about the young men and the shops. Catherine listened, and the morning passed very quickly.

'Tomorrow is Sunday,' Isabella said. 'In the morning, we will go to church. Then, we will walk together to the Royal Crescent.'

After that, Catherine and Isabella went everywhere together.

They liked clothes.

They liked theatres and balls.

And they read horror-stories.
They liked frightening stories!

Soon the two girls were very good friends.

3

John and James

Two weeks passed. It was Thursday morning. Catherine and Isabella were walking together in the streets of Bath.

'There are two young men in front of us,' Isabella said. 'They are looking at me. Let's walk on faster. Then we can pass them.'

Catherine was very surprised.

'Let's walk the other way,' she said.

'No, no!' Isabella replied. 'I want to show you a wonderful bookshop in Milsom Street. The shop sells books of horror-stories!'

The streets were crowded. There were hundreds of

people and there were many carriages.

Catherine and Isabella looked across the street. Suddenly, a small yellow carriage went past them. Isabella cried out.

'That is my brother, John!' she said. 'And your brother, James, is with him, Catherine!'

John Thorpe saw the two girls. He stopped the horse and he jumped down from the yellow carriage. His servant held the horse's reins.

John Thorpe was a fat young man with a plain face. He was not handsome. He turned and walked towards Catherine and Isabella. He bowed.

'John, this is Miss Morland, James' sister,' Isabella said.

'I'm very happy to meet you,' John Thorpe said, in a loud voice.

'Do you like my horse and carriage, Miss Morland?' John Thorpe asked. 'They are the best in Bath! I will take you for a drive one day.'

'We will enjoy a drive in your carriage, Mr Thorpe,' Catherine said.

'But four people cannot get into John's carriage,' said Isabella. 'I cannot come with you, Catherine.'

She smiled.

'No, Isabella, you cannot come with us,' John said rudely. 'James will take care of you.'

At that moment, James Morland walked up to them. James was tall and handsome. He smiled. 'Yes. I shall take care of Miss Thorpe,' he said.

Isabella laughed happily.

John Thorpe's servant drove the carriage away. The four young people walked along the street.

Soon, they came to Edgar's Buildings. Isabella spoke to James Morland. 'We have an apartment here,' she said. 'Please come in with your sister.'

The friends were together for an hour. John Thorpe talked to Catherine, and James Morland talked to Isabella.

'Shall we meet again tonight?' Isabella asked Catherine and James. 'There is a ball at the Upper Rooms.'

'Yes, let's meet tonight!' said John Thorpe. 'You will dance with me, Miss Morland.'

Catherine smiled. But she wanted to see Mr Tilney at the ball!

4

A Ball at the Upper Rooms

It was Thursday evening. James and Catherine Morland went to the Upper Rooms with Mrs Allen. They met Isabella Thorpe in the Upper Rooms. They all sat down in a large salon.

'Isabella, will you dance with me?' James asked.

'My brother is not here,' Isabella said. 'Catherine doesn't have a dancing-partner. I will wait until John comes.'

But a few minutes later, Isabella stood up.

'John will be here soon,' she said. 'I am going to dance with James now.'

Catherine Morland was unhappy. She was a pretty girl without a dancing-partner. She looked round the room. Suddenly, she saw Mr Tilney. But he had a beautiful young woman with him!

The young woman went towards some other people. Mr Tilney moved slowly across the room. He bowed to Catherine and Mrs Allen.

'I am very happy to see you again, Mr Tilney,' Mrs Allen said.

'My sister, Eleanor, is here with me tonight,' Mr Tilney said. Then he smiled at Catherine and he asked her to dance.

'I am very sorry,' Catherine said. 'But I am waiting for Mr Thorpe. I am going to dance with him.'

At that moment, John Thorpe came towards them. 'Now we will dance, Miss Morland,' he said.

At the end of the dance, John Thorpe left the room.

Isabella Thorpe walked up to Catherine.

'Your brother wants to dance with me again!' she said. 'But you must dance again too, my dear friend.'

Mr Tilney walked towards Catherine. 'Will you be my dancing-partner now?' he asked.

Catherine was very happy. She stood up and Mr Tilney held her hand. At that moment, John Thorpe came back into the room. He walked towards them.

'Miss Morland!' John Thorpe said. 'Why are you not dancing with me? Who is this man?'

'This is Mr Henry Tilney,' Catherine said. 'He wants to dance with me. You were not in the room.'

'I am Miss Morland's dancing-partner now,' Henry Tilney said. He spoke very politely. 'The dance is beginning. Please excuse us.'

John Thorpe was angry. He walked away.

Catherine and Mr Tilney started to dance.

'You have been in Bath for three weeks, Miss Morland,' said Mr Tilney. 'Are you bored? Or are you enjoying yourself?'

'Bath is not boring,' Catherine said.

'But your family is not in Bath?'

'My brother is here,' said Catherine. 'And I have some good friends.'

Mr Tilney smiled. 'My sister Eleanor will be your friend too,' he said.

A few minutes later, the dance ended. Catherine saw somebody looking at her. He was a tall, handsome old man.

Mr Tilney went towards the old man. He spoke with him. Then Henry Tilney walked back to Catherine.

'That man is my father, General Tilney,' he said. 'He was asking me your name.'

Catherine danced with Henry Tilney once more. Then Mr Tilney introduced her to his sister. Catherine sat down and Eleanor Tilney sat next to her. Eleanor was about twenty-two years old. She was beautiful and she was wearing a white dress.

'The country around Bath is very beautiful,' Eleanor Tilney said. 'Henry and I often walk in the country together. Please come with us one day. Please, come tomorrow!'

'Oh, yes,' Catherine replied. 'I am living with the Allens. They have an apartment in Pulteney Street. Let's meet there at twelve o'clock.'

Catherine had a another new friend. She was very happy.

5

'Why Did You Lie to Me?'

On Friday morning, Catherine woke early. She got out of bed and she looked out of the window. The sun was shining, but there were some clouds in the sky.

At about eleven o'clock, it started to rain.

'The Tilneys will not come,' she said sadly to Mrs Allen.

'The streets are wet,' Mrs Allen replied. 'But the clouds are going away. Soon, it will stop raining.'

At half-past twelve, the sun was shining again. Catherine was in a room upstairs. She looked out of the window. She saw two carriages coming along the street.

'Here is Isabella, with my brother and Mr Thorpe!' she said. 'But I cannot go out with them. I must wait for the Tilneys.'

Then Catherine heard a noise. Somebody was running up the stairs.

'Come quickly!' John Thorpe shouted. 'We are going to Blaize Castle, Miss Morland.'

'Blaize Castle? What is that?' Catherine asked.

'It is the oldest castle in England!'

'I cannot go,' Catherine said. 'I am waiting for Mr Tilney and his sister, Eleanor. We are going to walk in the country. They will be here soon, I am sure.'

'They are not coming,' John Thorpe said. 'I saw

them this morning. They were driving out of Bath.'

Catherine was very surprised. She did not say anything. But she believed John Thorpe's words.

Isabella came into the room.

'My dear Catherine, you must come with us,' she said. 'You will love Blaize Castle. It is old and very frightening! It is as frightening as a horror-story!'

A few minutes later, Catherine was sitting next to John Thorpe in his carriage. Isabella was with James Morland in the other carriage. The two carriages were going along Pulteney Street.

'Oh, stop, stop!' Catherine shouted. 'There are Mr Tilney and Miss Tilney. I must speak to them.'

John Thorpe laughed. But he did not stop the horse.

The Tilneys heard Catherine's voice. They stopped walking and they turned round.

'Why did you lie to me, Mr Thorpe?' Catherine asked. 'The Tilneys have not left Bath!'

John Thorpe laughed again. But he did not stop the horse.

At first, Catherine was sad about the Tilneys. Then she started to think about Blaize Castle. It was a very old building. Catherine liked horror-stories. The stories were about old buildings and their secrets. They were frightening stories. But Catherine liked frightening stories!

After two hours, James Morland shouted from his carriage. 'Stop, Thorpe! Stop!'

John Thorpe stopped his horse.

'What is wrong?' he asked.

'We must go back,' James replied. 'It's three o'clock. We cannot go to Blaize Castle today. It is too late. Blaize Castle is too far away.'

'We'll go back then. I don't care,' John Thorpe said.

So they drove back to Bath.

Catherine had dinner with the Thorpes. Then, after dinner, they all played cards.

Later, Catherine went back to Pulteney Street. Mrs Allen spoke to her.

'Mr Tilney and Miss Tilney came here this morning,' Mrs Allen said. 'They wanted to see you.'

Catherine was very unhappy. She went to bed and she cried.

6

Catherine and the Tilneys

The next day was Saturday. In the morning, Catherine spoke to Mrs Allen.

'I am going to visit Miss Tilney today,' Catherine said. 'I want to apologize to her. I want to tell her everything. I had to go with the Thorpes yesterday.'

'Yes, my dear. You must apologize. Go to Miss Tilney,' Mrs Allen said.

Catherine put on a new dress and a new hat. She went to Milsom Street. The Tilneys lived in a house in Milsom Street. But Miss Tilney was not at home.

That evening, Catherine and the Allens went to the theatre. The Tilneys were there too! Catherine did not watch the play. She looked at Henry Tilney. Once, he looked at her. But he did not smile.

At the end of the play, Mr Tilney came to speak to the Allens.

'Oh, Mr Tilney, I am very sorry,' Catherine said. 'I wanted to walk with you and your sister yesterday. But Mr Thorpe lied to me. He said, "The Tilneys have left Bath. I saw them this morning." But you had not left Bath. I saw you and Miss Tilney walking towards Pulteney Street.'

'Yes, we saw you too,' Henry Tilney said. 'But you did not stop.'

'I wanted to speak to you. But Mr Thorpe did not stop the carriage. Oh, I am very sorry, Mr Tilney!'

Henry Tilney smiled.

'My dear Miss Morland,' he said. 'We can walk in the country another day. Eleanor and I will take you to Beechen Cliff. There is a beautiful view of Bath from Beechen Cliff.'

On Sunday afternoon, Catherine and James walked along the Royal Crescent. Isabella and John Thorpe were there too.

Suddenly, Catherine saw Eleanor Tilney. She left her brother and the Thorpes and she walked towards Eleanor.

Isabella smiled at James.

'Mr Morland,' she said. 'Shall we all go to Blaize Castle tomorrow? We must leave Bath very early in the morning. What do you think?'

'That is a very good idea,' James replied. 'Do you agree, John?'

John Thorpe laughed. 'Yes, we must leave early. We must leave at nine o'clock,' he said.

'Good! We will go tomorrow morning,' Isabella said. 'Catherine wants to see Blaize Castle.'

Catherine had left Eleanor Tilney. She was walking towards her brother and the Thorpes.

'My dear Catherine,' Isabella said. 'Our brothers are going to take us to Blaize Castle tomorrow.'

'I cannot go tomorrow,' Catherine said quickly. 'I am going to walk to Beechen Cliff with the Tilneys.'

'No, no, we will go to Blaize Castle!' Isabella said. 'You can walk with the Tilneys another day. My dear Catherine, I am your friend. Miss Tilney is not your friend. You are making me very unhappy. You must come to Blaize Castle.'

Isabella started to cry. James saw her tears. He was angry with his sister.

'You are very unkind, Catherine,' he said. 'Isabella has been very kind to you.'

'Let's go to the Castle on Tuesday,' Catherine said.

'No, no!' John Thorpe said. 'On Tuesday, I am going back to Oxford.'

There was silence for a moment. Then Isabella spoke. She was very angry. 'I will not go to Blaize Castle without Catherine,' she said. 'Another woman must come with us.'

'John can take one of his other sisters,' Catherine

said. 'He can take Maria or Anne.'

'I do not want to take my sisters,' John Thorpe said. 'I want to take you, Catherine.' And he walked away.

Catherine, Isabella and James walked on for ten minutes. Nobody spoke. Then John Thorpe ran back.

'Everything is all right now, Catherine,' he said. 'I have spoken to the Tilneys. You will walk with them on Tuesday. Tomorrow, you will come with us.'

'That was a good idea,' Isabella said. She smiled.

'No, it was not a good idea,' Catherine said. 'I will follow Eleanor and I will speak to her myself.'

Catherine was very angry. She walked quickly, but the streets were very crowded. She could not see Eleanor. She ran along Milsom Street. The door of the Tilneys' house was open. Catherine did not stop. She went into the house and she ran up the stairs. She opened a door. Inside the room, Henry and Eleanor were speaking to their father.

'I am very sorry,' Catherine said quickly. 'I will not to go with the Thorpes tomorrow. I want to go with you to Beechen Cliff!'

'My dear Miss Morland, please sit down,' General Tilney said. 'You are welcome here.'

'Your message surprised me,' Eleanor said. 'But now I understand – the message was wrong. We can walk to Beechen Cliff tomorrow. Do you agree, Henry?'

Henry Tilney bowed and smiled at Catherine.

'I shall take you both,' he said.

Catherine enjoyed her visit to Beechen Cliff. Eleanor Tilney was a quiet girl. Henry Tilney was a clever young man. He talked well. Catherine liked Eleanor and Henry Tilney.

At the end of the afternoon, the Tilneys took Catherine back to Pulteney Street.

'Please come to dinner with us very soon,' Eleanor said. 'Can you come on Wednesday evening?'

'Yes!' said Catherine. And she was very happy.

7

Isabella Is in Love

The next Tuesday, a letter arrived for Catherine. It was from Isabella.

My dear Catherine,
Please come immediately. I must tell you something. I am waiting for you.
Your dear friend, Isabella

Catherine went to Edgar's Buildings. Isabella was eating her breakfast. She ran towards Catherine. She put her arms round her friend and laughed.

'Your dear, dear brother!' Isabella said. 'Oh, I am very excited! What will your parents say? Will they like me?'

'My dear Isabella!' Catherine said. 'What are you saying? Are you in love with James?'

'I am! I am!' said Isabella. 'And James is in love with me. He told me yesterday. I am very, very happy! I have always loved him! He is handsome and clever! Why did he choose me? I cannot understand it!'

'James is going to ride to your home in Fullerton today,' said Isabella. 'He is going to speak to your father. He is going to tell your father and mother about me. We want to get married. Will Mr and Mrs Morland agree?'

At that moment, James came into the room.

'Now you know everything, Catherine!' he said. 'I am a very happy man. Isabella, I am leaving Bath now. I shall write to you tonight.'

'Yes, go, dear James,' said Isabella. 'Go quickly! Come back to me soon!'

James' letter arrived a few days later. Catherine was with Isabella. All was well. Mr and Mrs Morland were happy. They had agreed to the marriage.

Isabella laughed and cried. 'James and I will get married soon,' she said.

John Thorpe had not gone back to Oxford. He was waiting for Isabella's news. Isabella showed him James' letter.

'James Morland is the best man in the world!' John Thorpe said. 'You will be very happy.'

Mrs Thorpe and Isabella wanted to tell the news to Maria and Anne. They left the room. John Thorpe was alone with Catherine.

'I must say goodbye to you, Miss Morland,' he said. 'I am leaving Bath today.'

He walked around the room. Then he spoke again.

'What do you think about this marriage? It is a good idea, isn't it?'

'Yes, I think it is,' Catherine said.

John Thorpe laughed. 'I know a song,' he said. He sang a few words – 'One wedding leads to another.' Then he asked, 'Will you be at Isabella's wedding?'

'Yes, I will be there,' Catherine replied.

'Then we can sing that song together, Miss Morland.'

Catherine did not understand. 'But I don't sing, Mr Thorpe,' she said. 'I must go now. Goodbye.'

'Wait, Miss Morland!' John Thorpe said. 'I shall be in Oxford for many weeks. But I want to see you again. I will come to Fullerton.'

'Then my family will meet you in Fullerton.'

'But will you meet me, Miss Morland?'

'Oh, I shall be in Fullerton,' Catherine said.

'That is good,' John Thorpe replied. 'Every man

wants a pretty wife and a big house. Don't you agree, Miss Morland?'

'Oh yes, Mr Thorpe. Goodbye.'

Catherine left the room. John Thorpe smiled.

'Yes,' he said to himself. 'Miss Morland is in love with me!'

8

Captain Frederick Tilney

It was Friday evening. Catherine was with the Allens and the Thorpes in the Upper Rooms.

'I will not dance!' Isabella said. 'James is not here. I will not dance with anybody else. I shall sit and think about my dear James.'

'Another letter from James arrived today,' Isabella said. 'We will get married, but we must wait for two years. After two years, James will leave Oxford. He will have a little money then.' Isabella spoke sadly.

Soon, Catherine saw the Tilneys. A tall man in uniform was with them. Henry introduced the man to Catherine.

'This is my brother, Captain Frederick Tilney,' he said.

Then Henry danced with Catherine. Catherine was happy. She was Henry's dancing-partner. For a few minutes, he talked and Catherine listened to him.

'Miss Thorpe will dance with Frederick,' said Henry.

'Oh no,' Catherine replied. 'Isabella is not going to dance tonight. James is not here. Isabella is going to get married to James. She will not dance with anybody tonight.'

'Won't she? Are you sure?' Henry asked. He smiled.

'Isabella said to me, "I will not dance with anybody tonight."'

'And you believed her!'

A few minutes later, Isabella was dancing with Captain Tilney. Catherine was very surprised.

At the end of the dance, Isabella sat next to Catherine.

'I am very tired!' Isabella said. 'And Captain Tilney talks so much. I did not want to dance.'

'Then why did you dance?' Catherine asked.

'Captain Tilney asked me to dance five times!' Isabella replied. 'I could not say no. He is a very handsome man. We danced. Everybody looked at us. I did not enjoy it. But James will come back to Bath soon. Then I shall be happy again.'

One evening, Catherine was at the Tilneys' house in Milsom Street. She had been in Bath for nearly six weeks.

'The time has passed very quickly!' Catherine said

to Eleanor Tilney. 'But I have good news. The Allens are staying for two more weeks. And I shall stay with them!'

'Oh,' Eleanor said. 'We are leaving at the end of next week. My father wants to go home to Northanger Abbey.'

'I am very sorry,' Catherine said. This was sad news.

'My father—' Eleanor said.

But at that moment, her father came into the room.

'Have you asked Miss Morland?' he said to Eleanor. 'Does she agree?'

'Catherine,' Eleanor said. 'My father – all of us – want you to come to Northanger Abbey. Will you come?'

Northanger Abbey! With Henry and Eleanor!

'Thank you!' Catherine said happily. 'You are very kind. I will write to my parents immediately.'

9

Isabella and James

On Monday, James Morland came back to Bath. On Tuesday morning, Catherine met Isabella in the Pump Room.

'Come and sit with me, dear Catherine,' Isabella said. 'I want to talk to you.'

They sat on a seat between two doors. Isabella looked first at one door, then at the other.

'James will be here soon,' Catherine said. She smiled.

'Why do you say that?' Isabella said. 'I am not looking for James. I am not looking for anybody.'

'But I have something to tell you,' Isabella said. 'I had a letter from John today. It is all about you.'

'The letter is about me?' Catherine said. She was surprised. 'Why is your brother writing about me?'

'My dear,' Isabella said. 'John is in love with you! He spoke to you about it – before he left Bath.'

'I do not understand!' Catherine said. 'There has been a mistake. I am sorry. But I cannot love him.'

Suddenly, Catherine saw Captain Tilney. He was walking towards them. He sat down next to Isabella.

'You are never alone,' he said. 'When will I see you alone?'

Isabella laughed. 'Why do you want to see me alone?' she asked. 'Tell me!'

Catherine was very surprised. Was Isabella in love with Captain Tilney? Isabella was going to marry James!

For the next three days, Catherine watched her friend carefully. Captain Tilney was always near Isabella. And she was always talking to him. She did not talk to James. James was very unhappy.

Catherine spoke to Henry Tilney.

'Please tell your brother about Isabella and James,' she said. 'They are going to get married.'

'Frederick knows about that,' Henry replied. 'I told him myself.'

'He must leave Bath,' Catherine said. 'He must not speak to Isabella. He is making James, my brother, very unhappy.'

'And Isabella?' Henry Tilney said. 'She talks to Frederick. She dances with him. She is making your brother unhappy too.'

'Yes, Isabella is wrong too,' Catherine said quietly.

'My brother will soon leave Bath,' said Henry. 'He will soon forget Isabella. James will be happy again.'

It was Catherine's last night in Bath. She and James had dinner with the Thorpes. Isabella was kind to James and he was happy. All was well.

The next morning, Mr Allen took Catherine to Milsom Street. The Tilneys were going to leave Bath at ten o'clock.

General Tilney's carriage went first. Eleanor sat with her father. Catherine Morland sat next to Henry in his carriage. They drove slowly out of Bath. Catherine was going to Northanger Abbey!

10

Northanger Abbey

The carriages travelled towards Northanger Abbey. Henry Tilney spoke to Catherine.

'My sister is happy,' said Henry. 'She is often alone at the Abbey. Now, you will be there with her.'

'But don't you live there?' Catherine asked.

'No,' Henry replied. 'I don't live there all the time. My home is at Woodston, twenty miles from Northanger Abbey. I am the clergyman of the church at Woodston.'

'Tell me about Northanger Abbey!' Catherine said. 'I have often read about abbeys. They are always old buildings, with lots of big dark rooms.'

'And there will be a big cupboard in your bedroom,' Henry said. 'You will try to open it. Then the flame of your candle will go out! And you will be alone, in the dark!' Henry was smiling.

'Oh, please, Mr Tilney, do not frighten me!' Catherine said.

It was a happy journey. Very soon, the travellers arrived at Northanger Abbey.

And then, Catherine was inside the Abbey. Eleanor took her upstairs. At last, Catherine was in her bedroom.

'Dinner will be at five o'clock,' Eleanor told her. 'I will come for you then.'

The dining-room was very large and the food was very good. General Tilney smiled and all was well. Catherine and the Tilneys had a happy evening.

At ten o'clock, Catherine went to her bedroom. The night was stormy. It was raining and the wind was blowing loudly.

Catherine looked round her bedroom. It was a fine room. She smiled.

'I like this house,' Catherine said to herself. 'It is different from the abbeys in horror-stories. The girls in horror-stories sleep in cold, dark rooms. But this is a fine room. I will look at everything before I go to bed.'

In one corner of the room, there was an old black cupboard. Catherine remembered Henry's words. The key was in the cupboard door and Catherine turned the key. At first, the door did not open. She turned the key again.

Then suddenly, the door opened. Catherine looked inside. Was the cupboard empty? No! There were some papers in the corner! Were they secret papers?

At that moment, the flame of Catherine's candle went out. The rain crashed against the windows. The wind made a terrible sound. Catherine remembered all the horror-stories about old abbeys. She was very frightened. Was somebody outside her door? Was somebody opening her window?

Catherine got into bed. She put her head under the bed-covers. She wanted to look at the writing on the papers in the cupboard. But she was too frightened. Was the writing on the papers about a terrible death – a murder? Was it about some jewels?

'I will look at the papers in the morning,' Catherine said to herself. At last, she fell asleep.

The next morning, Catherine woke up and got out of bed quickly. She ran towards the cupboard. She was excited! She was going to learn the terrible secret of Northanger Abbey!

Catherine picked up one of the papers and looked at it.

'Shirts. Stockings. Bed-covers,' she read. She picked up another paper. 'Three white shirts and two pairs of trousers.'

No terrible secrets! No jewels! The papers were lists of things for washing – laundry lists!

'I am very foolish,' Catherine said to herself. 'I have read too many horror-stories. I cannot tell Henry about the laundry lists. He will laugh at me.'

And Catherine went downstairs for breakfast.

11

'My Dear Miss Morland!'

Henry Tilney talked to Catherine at breakfast.

'It was a stormy night,' he said. Then he smiled. 'Did you sleep, Miss Morland? Were you frightened?'

'Oh, no,' Catherine replied quickly.

'I have to go to Woodston today,' Henry said. 'But my sister will be here with you.'

General Tilney always walked in the gardens after breakfast. 'Please walk with me,' he said to Catherine and Eleanor.

Some parts of Northanger Abbey were very old. Other parts were modern.

'I love old houses,' Catherine said. 'And the trees and hills are so beautiful here!'

The General was happy. He took Catherine and Eleanor into all the gardens. He showed them the fruit and the flowers. Eleanor, Catherine and the General were in the gardens for two hours.

At last, they started to walk back to the house. There was a path through some tall trees. Eleanor started to walk towards the path and Catherine followed her.

'I will not walk that way, Eleanor,' General Tilney said. 'The path is too wet.' He turned and walked away.

The two young women walked along the path. 'My

mother often walked here,' Eleanor said.

'But the General does not like this path,' Catherine said to herself. 'Why not?'

'Eleanor, is there a picture of your mother in the Abbey?' asked Catherine.

'Yes, I have a picture in my room,' Eleanor replied. 'My father does not like it.'

Catherine said nothing. She was thinking. The General did not want to see his wife's picture! Had he loved her? Or had he been a bad husband?

In the afternoon, the General, Eleanor and Catherine walked through the rooms of the Abbey. They walked through room after room. They looked at all the rooms downstairs. General Tilney talked about the furniture, the books and the paintings.

Then the General, Catherine and Eleanor went upstairs and they walked through some more rooms.

Eleanor walked towards an old door.

'Miss Morland has seen everything!' the General said quickly. 'Come downstairs, both of you!'

'That was my mother's room,' Eleanor said quietly.

'When did your mother die?' Catherine asked. 'Were you with her?'

'She died nine years ago,' Eleanor replied. 'She died very suddenly. I was not here. My father was with her.'

Catherine thought about Mrs Tilney. Had the General murdered his wife? Was she alive? Was she locked in a small, dark room? These things happened in horror-stories about old abbeys!

'I must see Mrs Tilney's room,' Catherine said to herself. 'That is the secret of Northanger Abbey!'

On Monday afternoon, Catherine went upstairs to her bedroom. Very quickly, she ran along to Mrs Tilney's room. She opened the door and she went into the room. She was surprised. The door was old but the room was modern. The room was not part of the old building. It was full of modern furniture. Catherine went out of the room and closed the door.

At that moment, she heard a noise. Somebody was coming up the stairs. It was Henry Tilney.

'What are you doing here?' Catherine asked.

'I have come from Woodston,' Henry replied. 'Have you been looking at my mother's room? Has Eleanor been talking about her?'

'Yes,' said Catherine. She spoke quickly. 'Your mother died very suddenly. She was alone with your father. Your father did not love her. Was your mother —?'

'My dear Miss Morland,' Henry said. 'What are you saying? I was here. The doctor was here. My father was very unhappy. He loved my mother very much. Miss Morland, you have read too many horror-stories!'

Catherine ran back to her room and cried.

'I have been very foolish,' she said to herself. 'I love Henry. But he will never love me now. I will never read a horror-story again.'

But Henry was very kind to Catherine that evening. Soon, she was happy again.

12

A Visit to Woodston

A week passed. On Thursday morning, Catherine was talking to Henry and Eleanor. A letter arrived for her. It was from James. He was in Oxford.

Oxford

Dear Catherine

I left Isabella in Bath yesterday. I will never see her again. She will not wait for me. She will not wait two years. She is going to marry Captain Tilney. Is he at Northanger Abbey? Please do not speak to him.

My dear sister, think carefully about people. Do not fall in love.

Your brother
James

Catherine read the letter. She started to cry.

'My dear Miss Morland!' Henry said. 'What is wrong?'

'Dear Catherine, can I help you?' Eleanor asked.

'James is very unhappy,' Catherine replied. 'Isabella Thorpe is not going to marry him. She is going to marry your brother, Captain Frederick Tilney. Please read the letter, both of you.'

'Isabella is not a good person,' Eleanor said. 'She has not been a good friend.'

On Saturday, Henry was going back to Woodston.

'We will all visit you next Wednesday, Henry,' General Tilney said. 'We will come at eleven o'clock.'

Catherine wanted to see Henry again. Sunday, Monday and Tuesday passed slowly. At last, Wednesday came. Catherine, Eleanor and General Tilney got into the General's carriage. Soon they were in the pretty village of Woodston.

The carriage stopped outside a modern house. Henry was waiting for them.

'Do you like my son's house, Miss Morland?' the General asked. 'It is not large. But it is big enough for a young man. Show Catherine all the rooms, Henry.'

Catherine liked the house very much. One of the rooms downstairs was empty.

'What a pretty room!' Catherine said. 'You can see the garden from this big window. It is a beautiful view.

Why don't you use this room, Mr Tilney? It is the best room in the house.'

The General smiled.

'One day, there will be a lady in the house,' he said. And he smiled again.

'Now show us the garden, Henry,' he said.

Catherine was very happy. The General wanted her to marry Henry. But what did Henry think? Catherine did not know.

Everybody walked in the garden. Catherine liked everything – every flower and every tree. She walked happily next to Henry.

Later, Catherine and the Tilneys looked at Henry's horses. Then they walked through the village. After that, they had dinner.

Soon, it was time to go.

'Have you enjoyed your visit, Miss Morland?' the General asked. 'Do you like my son's house?'

'Oh, yes,' Catherine replied. 'I like it very much.'

'Will you come again?' the General asked. 'You will always be welcome here – and at Northanger Abbey.'

Catherine did not speak. But she understood.

'General Tilney likes me,' she said to herself. 'But does Henry love me? Does he want to marry me?'

13

A Letter from Isabella

On Friday morning, two things happened. Henry came back to Northanger Abbey and a letter arrived for Catherine. The letter was from Isabella.

My dearest Catherine,

My family will leave Bath tomorrow. I hate this place. All my friends have left. James is in Oxford, but he has not written to me. Why not? I will never love anybody else.

Catherine, please write to James. Did I make him unhappy? I do not know. Will he write to me? Then everything will be well again.

Another man has left Bath too – Captain Tilney. I hate him. I often saw him, but I never liked him. I only like your dear brother.

I never go to balls now, but I went to the theatre last night. I must enjoy myself sometimes.

Please, please write to your brother. And write to me too.

Your loving friend,
Isabella

Catherine showed the letter to Eleanor and Henry.

'I understand,' Catherine said. 'Captain Tilney did not love Isabella. She will be sad.'

'No, Miss Morland,' Henry said. 'Isabella will not be sad. She did not love my brother, Frederick. They were both wrong. Write to your brother, James. Forget Isabella Thorpe.'

The next day was Saturday. General Tilney went to London. But Henry stayed at Northanger Abbey. 'I will go back to Woodston next Saturday,' he said.

Catherine was happy. She was with her two dear friends.

14

Catherine Goes Home

It was Thursday.

'Eleanor, I have been at Northanger Abbey for four weeks,' Catherine said. 'I must go home.'

'Oh, please do not go!' Eleanor said.

'Do stay, Miss Morland,' Henry said. He smiled at Catherine.

Catherine was happy. 'Yes, Henry loves me,' she said to herself.

On Saturday, Henry went back to Woodston. Catherine and Eleanor were together all day. Late in the evening, Catherine was in her bedroom. She was reading a book.

She heard a sound outside her room. She went to the door and opened it. Eleanor was standing there. Her face was white.

'What is wrong?' Catherine asked.

'Oh, how can I tell you? How can I tell you?' Eleanor said.

'Has something happened at Woodston?' Catherine asked.

'No, no. My father has come back,' said Eleanor. 'Catherine, we are leaving Northanger Abbey on Monday. We are going to visit some friends. You must go back to Fullerton tomorrow. I am sorry, Catherine.'

'Tomorrow!' Catherine said.

Eleanor started to cry.

'Have I done something wrong?' Catherine asked.

'No, no. But my father is very angry,' said Eleanor.

Catherine did not sleep well that night. She woke very early. At six o'clock, Eleanor came into her bedroom.

'My father's carriage will take you home,' Eleanor said. 'You must leave at seven o'clock.'

Catherine did not eat any breakfast. She was very sad. Soon the carriage was at the door.

'I will write to you, Eleanor,' Catherine said. 'Please tell Henry—'

But Catherine could not say any more. She ran to the carriage. Soon, she had left Northanger Abbey.

15

'Will You Marry Me?'

Catherine sat in General Tilney's carriage. She cried and cried.

'The General was very kind to me last week,' Catherine thought. 'Why is he angry with me now?'

The journey to Fullerton was very long. Catherine travelled for eleven hours. At about six o'clock in the evening, Catherine saw her father's house.

Catherine's parents were very surprised. But they were very happy. Then Catherine told them everything.

'It is very strange,' Mrs Morland said. 'Why did you have to leave Northanger Abbey? I am sorry. But you are home again now, Catherine. Forget the Tilneys.'

Catherine did not want to forget the Tilneys. The next day, she wrote to Eleanor. And she sent Henry her best wishes.

'You will not see the Tilneys again,' Mrs Morland said. 'And James is not going to be married. It is very strange!'

Three days passed. Catherine was very unhappy. And then the Morlands had a visitor – Mr Henry Tilney! Mr and Mrs Morland were very surprised. But Mrs Morland said, 'My daughter's friends are always very welcome here.'

Catherine did not say anything. But she was very, very happy. Henry was here – here to see her!

'Will you walk with me in the garden?' Henry Tilney asked.

'Yes,' said Catherine, quietly.

Soon Henry and Catherine were alone. Henry's first words were of love.

'I want to ask you a question,' he said. 'I love you, Catherine. Will you marry me? Please give me your answer.'

Catherine could not say anything. But Henry knew her answer. They walked on happily.

'What will your father say?' Catherine asked. 'General Tilney sent me away from his house. Why?'

'I went back to the Abbey last Monday,' Henry said. 'You were not there. I spoke to my father. "You must never see Catherine again," my father said.'

'But I have done nothing wrong,' Catherine said.

'No, you have done nothing wrong,' said Henry. 'I will tell you everything.' He smiled at Catherine.

'My father likes rich people,' he said. 'My father spoke to John Thorpe in Bath.'

'John Thorpe?' Catherine said. 'What did he tell your father about me?'

'John Thorpe said, "Miss Morland's father is very rich. And the Allens have money too. They will give it to Miss Morland." Those were his words,' said Henry.

'But my father is not very rich,' said Catherine. 'And the Allens are not going to give me any money.'

'I know that,' said Henry. 'John Thorpe lied to my father. But my father heard the truth in London. John Thorpe told him the truth. My father was very angry and he sent you away from Northanger Abbey.'

'The Thorpes were bad friends,' Catherine said. 'But what did you say to your father?'

'I told him about my love for you. I do not care about money. I went back to Woodston. And then I came here.'

'And I am very happy!' Catherine said. 'We must tell my parents everything now.'

Henry spoke to Mr Morland.

'Sir, I want to marry Catherine,' he said.

Mr and Mrs Morland were happy. They liked Henry Tilney.

'But will General Tilney agree to the marriage?' Mr Morland asked.

Henry went back to Northanger Abbey. A few days later, a letter arrived from Eleanor.

My dear Catherine,

I have some good news. I am going to get married in the summer. The young man is very handsome and very rich. My father is very happy.

Henry has spoken to Father about you. Father has agreed to your marriage too. Let's be married on the same day, my dear Catherine! Henry will write to you soon.

Your dearest friend,
Eleanor Tilney

Catherine told her parents immediately. They were as happy as their daughter.

One day in the summer, Catherine got married to Henry Tilney. Eleanor and her rich young man got married at the same time. And General Tilney smiled at everybody.

It was a happy day.

Heinemann English Language Teaching
A division of Reed Educational and Professional Publishing Limited
Halley Court, Jordan Hill, Oxford OX2 8EJ

OXFORD MADRID FLORENCE ATHENS PRAGUE
SÃO PAULO MEXICO CITY CHICAGO PORTSMOUTH (NH)
TOKYO SINGAPORE KUALA LUMPUR MELBOURNE
AUCKLAND JOHANNESBURG IBADAN GABORONE

ISBN 0 435 27339 6

This retold version for Heinemann Guided Readers

First published 1997

Acknowledgements: The publishers would like to thank Popperfoto for permission to reproduce the picture on page 4.

Illustrated by Alexy Pendle. Map on page 3 by John Gilkes
Typography by Adrian Hodgkins
Designed by Sue Vaudin
Cover by Sarah Ball and Marketplace Design
Typeset in 12/16 Goudy
Printed and bound in Malta by Interprint Limited

97 98 99 00 10 9 8 7 6 5 4 3 2 1